DEDICATION

TO HATTIE

This book is dedicated to Hattie Elizabeth. During the 14 years I shared with her, she taught me the most important thing in life is to treat every day as a gift.
Be a hero and save a life.
Adopt a shelter pet.

Always Dream Big!
Connie & Charlotte

Published by Tails and Tales, LLC

Printed by Oswego Printing Company, Inc.
Oswego, New York

ISBN # 978-0-9832626-5-7

Charlotte's Big Dream

Written by Connie Evans

Illustrated by Jim Arnold

Published by Tails and Tales, LLC

As far back as Charlotte could remember, she had dreamed of having a home of her very own.

5

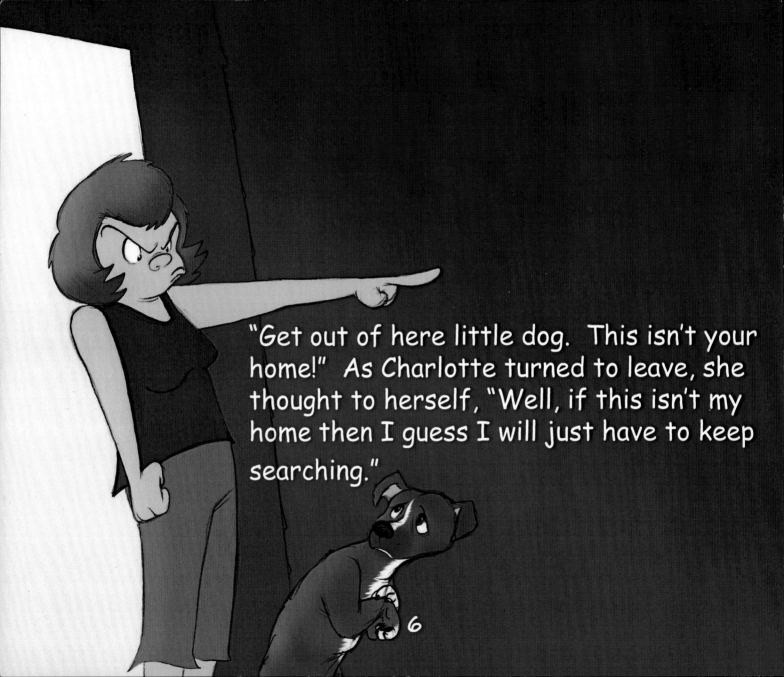

"Get out of here little dog. This isn't your home!" As Charlotte turned to leave, she thought to herself, "Well, if this isn't my home then I guess I will just have to keep searching."

"Someday I will have a home of my own and maybe, just maybe, a warm, comfy bed."

"I'm so hungry maybe I can find something in here to eat." As Charlotte dug through the trash can, she thought to herself, "Someday I will have a home of my own with a warm comfy bed and maybe, just maybe plenty of food and fresh water."

As the sun rose the next day Charlotte thought, "Today could be the day I find my new home."

As Charlotte continued searching for her new home she found an old shoe. As she tossed it in the air she thought to herself, "Someday I will have a home of my

own, with a warm comfy bed, plenty of food and fresh water, and maybe, just maybe, a toy to play with."

Charlotte watched as a woman and her dog walked by. The dog looked so happy. The dog was wearing a beautiful collar with her name on it. The dog was clean and smelled so nice. As they walked by, Charlotte thought,

"Someday I will have a home of my own, with a warm comfy bed, plenty of food and fresh water, a toy of my very own, and maybe, just maybe, a pretty leash and collar with my name on it."

As Charlotte walked through the park, she noticed other dogs playing ball. "I love to play ball! Can I play too?" Charlotte and the other dogs played for hours, but then they had to go home. Charlotte was sad to see the dogs leave because she knew she didn't have a home to go to.

That night she dreamt of a day when she had a home of her own, a warm comfy bed, plenty of food and fresh water, a toy of her own, a collar with her name on it and maybe, just maybe, a doggie brother or sister.

The next day, Charlotte searched high and low for her new home. She thought, "I am so very tired and hungry and I have been searching for my home for such a long time. I wish someone would help me."

That night Charlotte was too tired to dream. She just curled up and fell asleep.

Just then a car pulled up and a lady got out and said, "You look like you could use some help." Charlotte asked, "Could you please help me find my new home?"
"Sure" the lady said, "I will help you but first we need to take you to see the veterinarian and get you all fixed up."

Charlotte thought, "What is a veterinarian? I've never heard of that." The rescue lady smiled and said, "It's a doctor for animals."

The lady took Charlotte to see the doctor.
They gave her medicine to make her feel
better and fixed her boo-boos.
They gave her food and water.

After Charlotte ate a good meal, she felt much better. The rescue lady and the doctor told Charlotte they would both help her find a new home.

That night Charlotte dreamt of a home of her own, with a warm comfy bed, plenty of food and fresh water, a toy of her own, a collar with her name on it, and maybe, just maybe, a doggie brother or sister of her very own.

23

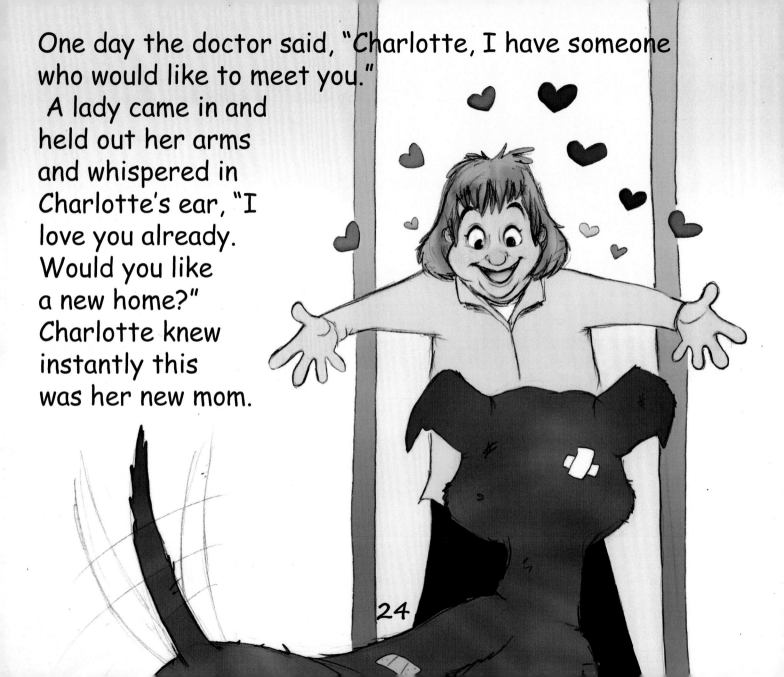

One day the doctor said, "Charlotte, I have someone who would like to meet you."
A lady came in and held out her arms and whispered in Charlotte's ear, "I love you already. Would you like a new home?" Charlotte knew instantly this was her new mom.

24

Charlotte wanted to yell, "Yes! Yes please take me home," but at that very moment all she could do was close her eyes and cuddle into her new mom's arms. There would be time for talking later. Right now Charlotte was just happy to be loved.

As Charlotte pulled up in front of a little white house she could see her new brothers and sisters waving at her.

She could see her new yard where she could play
with her new toy. "This is it, this is my home!"

As Charlotte drifted off to sleep that night in her new home, curled up in her warm comfy bed , with a full belly, her toy tucked beneath one paw, wearing her new collar with her name on it, her brothers and sisters cuddled around her, she realized all of her dreams had come true. She thought to herself, "What will I dream of next?"